Introduction

Welcome to your all-inclusive guide to the world of lavish Victorian crazy quilts and t. them so memorable. This extensive volume features over **75 delightful stitches and n** when crazy quilt artistry was at its peak in the 1880's.

Inspired by Victorian opulence, genteel women of those days indulged in collecting small pieces of sumptuous fabrics to arrange in unique mosaics. They then skillfully covered the random patches and seams with embroidery and other embellishments.

Now you can create your own nostalgic showpieces, beginning with our easy-to-finish little quilts and pillows. The design possibilities are endless, and you'll enjoy using this handy resource again and again!

Contents

The Paper-Pieced Block

A single block made from six different fabrics is used for each of the glorious projects. Using speedy paper piecing to complete your blocks will leave you more time for the fun part – embroidering!

How To Paper Piece Your Block

1. Make **reversed** photocopies of Block pattern, pg. 2. Any copy shop can do this for you. Make one copy for each block you plan to piece.

> *Pat's Pointer: If you are using fabrics with significantly different weights, or ones that ravel easily, you may wish to piece your blocks onto muslin foundations. Simply trace the **reversed** pattern onto muslin, then treat it like a paper pattern, except that you don't remove the foundation when piecing is complete.*

2. Label fabrics A-F to match sections on block pattern. Use the non-reversed block pattern as a guide to roughly cut out one fabric piece for each area of the pattern. Pieces should be at least 1/2" larger on all sides than the corresponding section on the block.

3. Place reversed photocopy, face up, in front of a light source. On wrong side of photocopy, center fabric piece A on Section A with right side of fabric facing out. Make sure that fabric extends beyond all section A seamlines; pin in place.

4. Place fabric piece B on top of A, with right sides together. Use your light source to check that when you sew A and B pieces together along the line separating those sections, that fabric piece B will completely cover section B on the photocopy when it is opened up. Once adjusted, place photocopy, fabric side down, under your sewing machine needle. Using a short straight stitch, sew directly on top of line separating sections A and B. Turn paper over and trim fabric seam allowance to 1/4". Open fabric piece B and press; pin in place.

5. Repeat Step 4 to add remaining fabric pieces to photocopy.

6. Using a medium stitch length, stay-stitch along outer solid lines of block.

7. Trim excess fabric on dotted line to complete block. Tear away photocopy.

> *Pat's Pointer: You may wish to trim the outer edges of your blocks to 1/2" instead of the standard 1/4" if you have fabrics that tend to ravel or if you plan to finish your project by adding a ruffle or welting.*

©2009 by Leisure Arts, Inc., 5701 Ranch Drive, Little Rock, AR 72223-9633
www.leisurearts.com

 PRINTED WITH SOY INK

 Made in U.S.A.

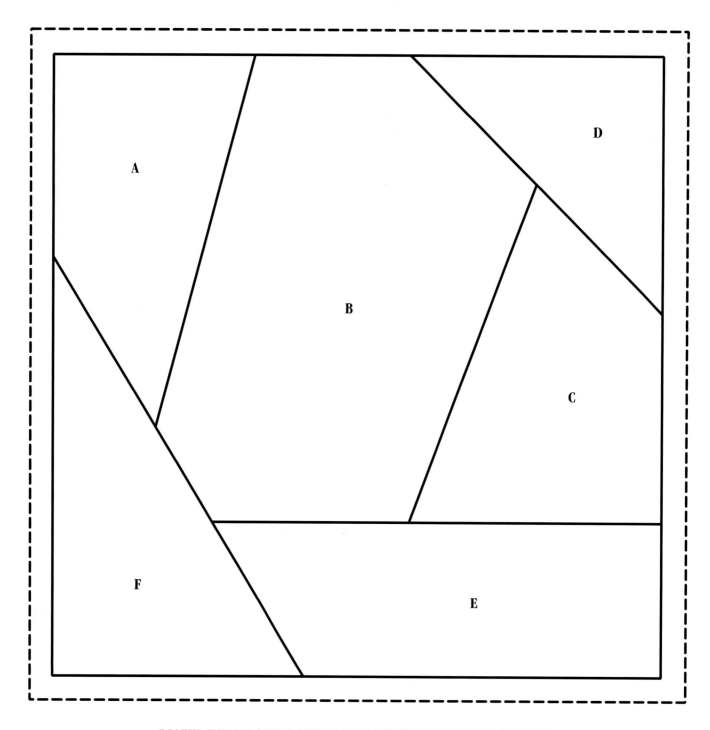

MAKE *REVERSED* COPIES FOR FOUNDATION PATTERNS.

Leisure Arts gives permission to the owner of this book to photocopy this page for personal use only.

3

The Embroidered Block

Taking the single pieced block as a base, rotating it, and then adding beautiful designs creates five very different blocks. Each block features a key so you can look up any stitches that are new to you in the stitch diagrams (pg. 9).

Transferring the Design to the Block

Pat's Pointer: *Transferring the design to your fabric doesn't have to be a big deal. Transfer as few lines to the fabric as possible, just so you know where to place the major components of the design.*

Method 1: For light-colored fabrics, use a light source, such as a light table or a window, to simply trace the design onto the fabric using a pencil.

Method 2: For dark-colored fabrics or fabrics that you don't want to risk leaving permanent marks on, trace design onto a piece of heat-sensitive brush-off fabric stabilizer or water-soluble fabric stabilizer (available at fabric stores) using a permanent fine-point pen. Baste the stabilizer onto the right side of the block. Embroider design, stitching through stabilizer. When stitching is complete, remove basting threads and stabilizer.

Block 1

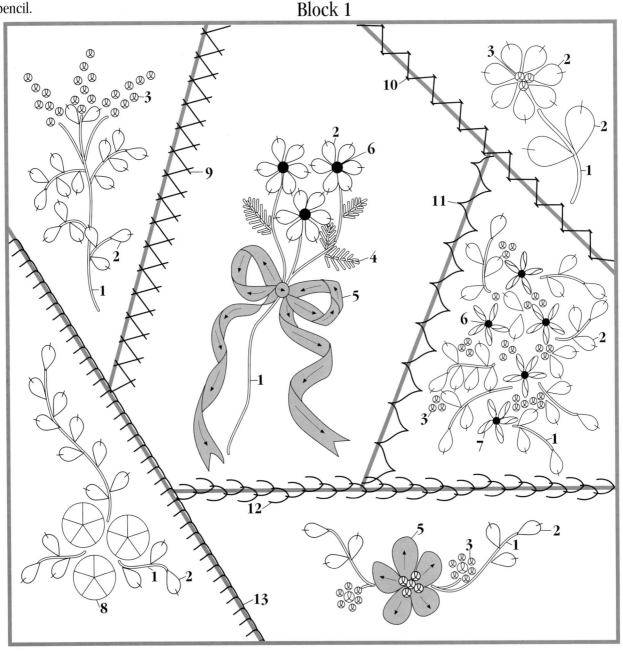

BLOCK 1 KEY

1 – Stem Stitch	5 – Satin Stitch	9 – Herringbone Stitch
2 – Lazy Daisy	6 – Bead or French Knot	10 – Chevron Stitch
3 – French Knot or bead	7 – Wrapped Straight Stitch	11 – Cretan Stitch
4 – Fishbone Stitch	8 – Woven Rose	12 – Feather Stitch
		13 – Blanket Stitch

Block 2

BLOCK 2 KEY

1 – Stem Stitch	5 – Closed Cretan Stitch	9 – Woven Rose
2 – Straight Stitch	6 – Bead or French Knot	10 – Fly Stitch
3 – French Knot or bead	7 – Satin Stitch	11 – Blanket Stitch Variation
4 – Lazy Daisy	8 – Buttonhole Wheel	12 – Cross Stitch Star Variation

Block 3

BLOCK 3 KEY

1 – Stem Stitch

2 – Straight Stitch

3 – Lazy Daisy

4 – Bead or French Knot

5 – Woven Rose

6 – Satin Stitch

7 – French Knot or bead

8 – Buttonhole Wheel

9 – Blanket Stitch Variation

10 – Fishbone Stitch

11 – Chain Stitch

12 – Woven Running Stitch

13 – Cross Stitch

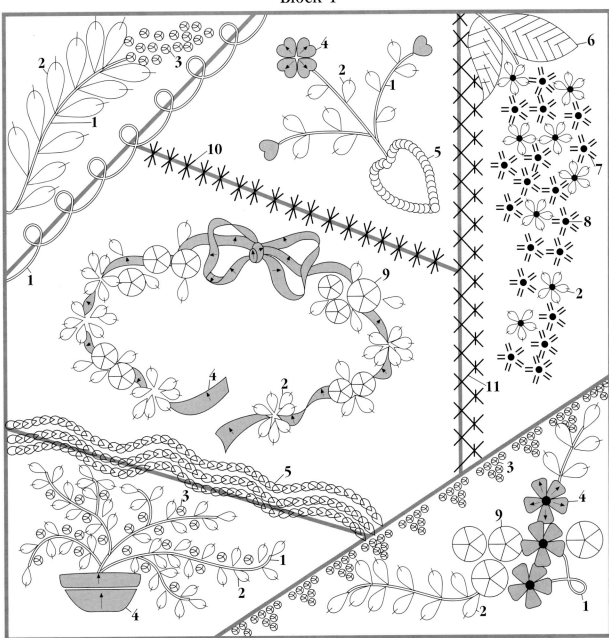

BLOCK 4 KEY

1 – Stem Stitch

2 – Lazy Daisy

3 – French Knot or bead

4 – Satin Stitch

5 – Chain Stitch

6 – Closed Cretan Stitch

7 – Straight Stitch

8 – Bead or French Knot

9 – Woven Rose

10 – Cross Stitch Star Variation

11 – Herringbone Variation

Block 5

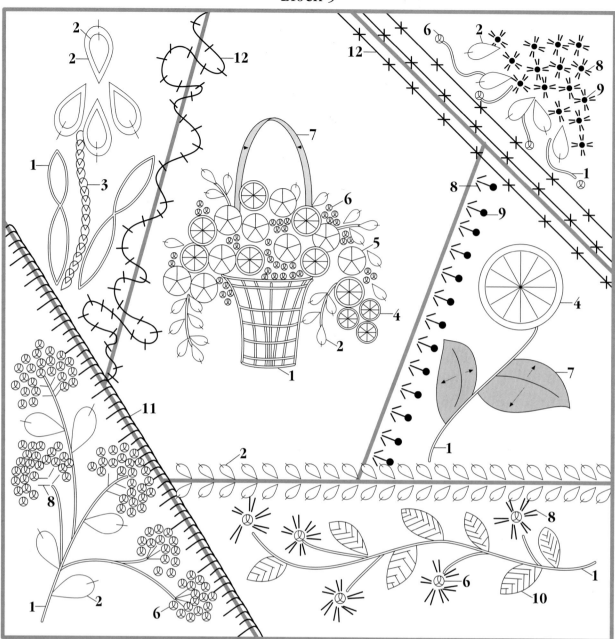

BLOCK 5 KEY

1 – Stem Stitch

2 – Lazy Daisy

3 – Chain Stitch

4 – Buttonhole Wheel

5 – Woven Rose

6 – French Knot or bead

7 – Satin Stitch

8 – Straight Stitch

9 – Bead or French Knot

10 – Closed Cretan Stitch

11 – Blanket Stitch Variation

12 – Couching

The Embroidery Stitches

Most of the projects are stitched using cotton embroidery floss. You can markedly change the look of a stitch (and thus your project) by changing the number of strands you use. We've included a range of floss strands with each of the stitch diagrams to help you decide how many strands might work well for your project.

Blanket Stitch – Use 2 or 3 strands of floss

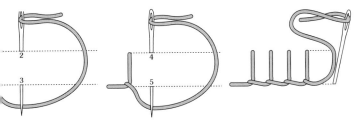

Blanket Stitch Variation – Use 2 or 3 strands of floss

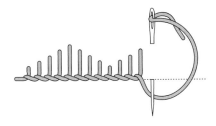

Buttonhole Wheel – Use 3 to 6 strands of floss

Chain Stitch – Use 2 or 3 strands of floss

Chevron Stitch – Use 3 strands of floss

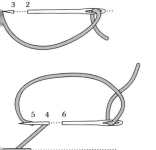 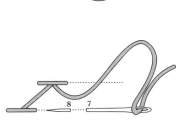

Closed Cretan – Use 2 or 3 strands of floss

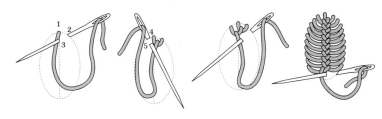

Couching – Lay 6 or 12 strands and use 3 strands to stitch over the laid thread

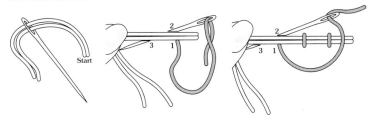

Cretan Stitch – Use 3 strands of floss

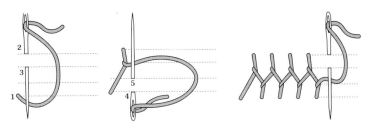

Cross Stitch – Use 2 or 3 strands of floss

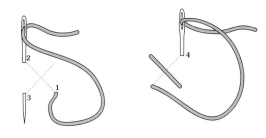

Cross Stitch Star Variation – Use 2 or 3 strands of floss

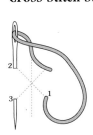  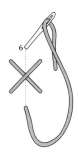

Continued on pg. 12

Feather Stitch – Use 2 or 3 strands of floss

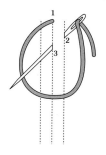 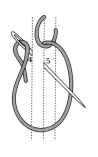 

Fishbone Stitch – Use 2 or 3 strands of floss

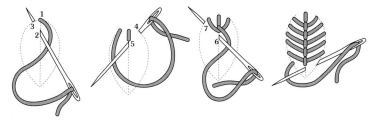

Fly Stitch – Use 2 or 3 strands of floss

French Knot – Use 3 to 12 strands of floss

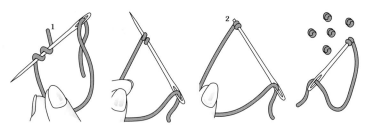

Herringbone Stitch – Use 2 or 3 strands of floss

Herringbone Variation – Use 2 or 3 strands of floss

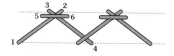

Lazy Daisy – Use 2 to 6 strands of floss

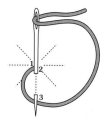 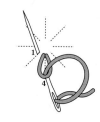 

Running Stitch – Use 2 or 3 strands of floss

Satin Stitch – Use 2 or 3 strands of floss

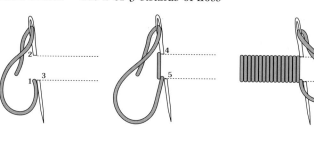

Stem Stitch – Use 2 or 3 strands of floss

Straight Stitch – Use 3 to 6 strands of floss

Woven Rose – Use 2 strands of floss for spokes, and 6 strands of floss for weaving

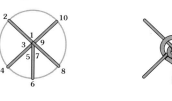

Woven Running Stitch – Use 2 or 3 strands of floss

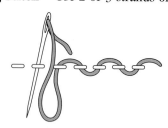

Wrapped Straight Stitch – Use 3 to 6 strands of floss

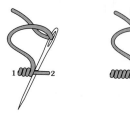

The Projects

Whether you choose to duplicate a project given here or create your own embroidered heirloom, this showcase of five enticing designs will inspire you to pull out your fabrics and floss and start stitching!

Precious Purple Pillow
(Photo, pg. 3)

Supplies
Fabrics
    6 different scraps of purple cottons
    7½" square for backing
Floss
    3 greens, 2 pinks, purple, yellow, ecru
Embellishments
    Lace trims
    Antique buttons
    Ecru satin ribbon
    Seed beads for fringe trim – purple and pink
Other supplies
    Fiberfill
    Beading needle
    Nylon thread

Description
One paper-pieced block (pg. 2) was embroidered using some of the designs from Block 1 (pg. 4). No seam-covering stitches were used. Lace trims were stitched along two seams, and buttons and a bow were stitched to unembroidered areas. The block was made into a knife-edge pillow (pg. 19), and a beaded fringe was added.

Technique – Beaded Fringe
1. Thread beading needle with 18" length of nylon thread. Take several small stitches at one corner of pillow to secure thread.

2. Thread 7 purple, 3 pink, and 1 purple bead onto thread. Skip last bead on thread, then thread needle back through pink beads. Thread 7 more purple beads onto thread. Take a small stitch in seamline of pillow about ³/₈" from first stitch.

Beaded Fringe Diagram

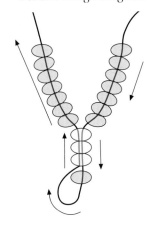

3. Continue to repeat sequence around entire edge of pillow.

Ring Bearer's Pillow
(Photo, pg. 3)

> **Pat's Pointer:** *Here's the perfect project for using fabrics leftover from the wedding gown! Use a very "limp" fabric for the pillow ruffle to ensure the most beautiful drape.*

Supplies
Fabrics
    6 different scraps of white and ecru bridal specialty fabrics
    ¼ yd for welting and backing
    ½ yd for ruffle
Floss
    2 beiges, ecru, pink, green
Embellishments
    Ecru seed beads
    Narrow satin ribbon
    2 wedding ring favors
Other supplies
    1 yd of ⅛" cotton cord for welting
    Fiberfill

Description
One paper-pieced block (pg. 2) was embroidered using Block 2 (pg. 5), omitting Section B. The block was made into a welted pillow with a 3" finished ruffle (pg. 20). The satin ribbon was used to tie the wedding ring favors to Section B.

Jewel-tone Pillow
(Photo, pg. 3)

> **Pat's Pointer:** *Add variety to your work by adding a single strand of another floss color to your primary floss. I mixed 1 strand of dark pink with 2 strands of light pink when stitching the buttonhole and lazy daisy flowers on this pillow.*

Supplies
Fabrics
    6 jewel-tone cottons (¼ yd each) – 3 purples, magenta, blue, green
    1 yd for welting and backing
Floss
    3 pinks, 3 greens, 2 beiges, brown, purple, blue
Embellishments
    Pink and blue seed beads
    4" crocheted doily
    Antique buttons
    Narrow purple satin ribbon
Other supplies
    Fiberfill
    1½ yds of ¼" cord for welting

13

Continued on pg. 15

Description

Four paper-pieced blocks (pg. 2) were sewn together for the pillow top. Elements of Blocks 2-5 (pgs. 5-8) were embroidered, leaving the center of the pillow top unstitched. Ribbon was threaded through the doily and tied into a bow. The doily and buttons were sewn to the pillow top. It was made into a welted pillow (pg. 20).

Beautiful Blue Wall Hanging
(Photos, front cover and pg. 14)

Supplies
Fabrics
    6 blue and white cottons (1/2 yd each)
    1 yd for border and binding
    1 yd for backing
Floss
    4 pinks, 4 greens, 2 olive greens, 2 blues, 2 yellows,
        2 purples
Embellishments
    Seed beads – green, yellow, pink, purple iridescent,
        dark blue
    2 1/2 yds of flat lace trim
Other supplies
    30" square of low-loft batting

Description
Nine paper-pieced blocks (pg. 2) were embroidered using Blocks 1-5 (pgs. 4-8). The blocks were sewn into three rows of three. It was made into a wall hanging.

Technique - Wall Hanging Finishing
Use a 1/4" seam allowance unless noted.

1. Cut four 3 3/4" x 26 1/2" border strips. Center and pin one border strip to top of quilt top. Beginning and ending 1/4" from edges of quilt top, stitch border strip in place. Repeat for each strip.

2. Fold one corner of quilt top diagonally, matching edges. Use a ruler to mark diagonal seamline. Pin, then stitch borders together along drawn line. Trim seam allowance to 1/4" and press. Repeat for each corner.

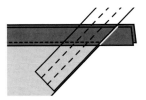 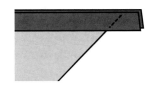

3. Stitch lace trim to inner edge of border.

4. Layer and baste backing, batting, and quilt top together (pg. 19).

5. Hand quilt (pg. 19) 1/4" inside edges of Section B on each block.

6. Bind quilt (pg. 19) using a 3 1/4"w bias strip and a 1/2" seam allowance.

7. Cut a 3" x 25" piece of backing fabric for hanging sleeve. Press edges 1/2" to wrong side. Slipstitch long edges to top center back of wall hanging.

Baby's Comforter
(Photo, pg. 10)

Supplies
Fabrics
    Pastel juvenile-print cotton or poly/cotton (about 2 yds. You
        may need more or less fabric depending on how the motifs
        on your fabric are spaced.)
    5 pastel cottons (1/2 yd each) – yellow, blue, pink, green,
        purple
    1 yd for narrow border and binding
    1 yd for wide border
    1 yd for backing
Floss
    Yellow, blue, pink, green, purple
Other supplies
    Crib-size low-loft batting

Continued on pg. 16

Description

Twenty blocks were paper-pieced (pg. 2), using the juvenile print for Section B on each block. The blocks were sewn together in five rows of four blocks each. Seam-covering stitches from Blocks 1-5 (pgs. 4-8) were embroidered on blocks. A feather stitch was worked along seamlines between the blocks. It was made into a tied quilt.

Technique - Tied Quilt Finishing
Use a ¹/₄" seam allowance unless noted.

1. Cut two 1¹/₄" x 26¹/₂" and two 1¹/₄" x 34¹/₂" strips of narrow border fabric. Cut two 3³/₄" x 28" and two 3³/₄" x 40¹/₂" strips of wide border fabric.

2. Sew top, bottom, then side narrow borders to embroidered piece. Sew wide borders in the same order.

3. Layer and pin-baste backing, batting, and quilt top together (pg. 19).

4. To tie quilt, thread a large needle with 2 yd lengths of pink, blue, and yellow floss. Working from the front of the quilt, take needle down through all layers near corner of one block. Come up in corner of diagonal block. Cut floss, leaving 6" tails. Repeat for all block intersections. Thread needle with 2 yd lengths of yellow, green, and purple floss. Repeat stitching process, coming up at opposite corners of block intersections. Holding two groups of floss together, make a double knot on top of quilt, pulling floss snug. Trim floss ends to about 1".

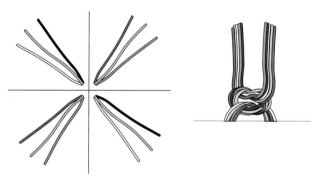

5. Machine quilt (pg. 19) in the ditch along both long edges of narrow border.

6. Bind quilt (pg. 19) using 3¹/₄"w bias strip and a ¹/₂" seam allowance.

Warm Woolen Throw
(Photo, back cover)

Pat's Pointer: *The extra sheen of pearl cotton complements the woolens used in this throw. You can substitute pearl cotton for regular embroidery floss for almost any stitch. Use a single strand for stitching and a doubled strand for couched stitches.*

Supplies
Fabrics
    6 wool fabrics (1 yd each) – black, purple, 2 greens, 2 plaid
    1¹/₂ yds for narrow border
    1³/₄ yds for wide border and binding
    1¹/₄ yds for backing (60"w)
Floss
    Black, blue, purple, blue green, 2 yellows, 3 olive greens
#5 pearl cotton
    Purple, red, blue green
Other supplies
    Twin-size low-loft batting

Description

Thirty-five paper-pieced blocks (pg. 2) were sewn together in seven rows of five blocks each to make the quilt top. Section B and the seam-covering stitches from Blocks 1-5 (pgs. 4-8) were embroidered on the blocks. A feather stitch was worked along seamlines between the blocks. It was made into a tied quilt.

Technique – Tied Quilt Finishing
Use a ¹/₄" seam allowance unless noted.

1. Cut two 2" x 33" and two 2" x 49" strips of narrow border fabric. Cut two 3³/₄" x 36" and two 3³/₄" x 55¹/₂ " strips of wide border fabric.

2. Sew top, bottom, then side narrow borders to embroidered piece. Sew wide borders in the same order.

3. Layer backing, batting, and quilt top together (pg. 19).

4. To tie quilt, thread needle with a 2 yd length of red pearl cotton. Follow Step 4 of Baby's Comforter (this page) to tie quilt at each corner of each block.

5. Bind quilt (pg. 19) using 3¹/₄"w bias strip and a ¹/₂" seam allowance.

SPECIAL BONUS - Silk Ribbon Embroidery

Silk ribbon comes in various widths. Though it can be used for many standard embroidery stitches, several unique and easy stitches have been developed that show off the ribbon's beautiful drape and texture.

Working with Silk Ribbon

Threading Needle with Ribbon: Thread needle with a 14" length of ribbon. Pierce ribbon with point of needle, about 1/4" from end. Pull short end of ribbon back down over ribbon; gently tug long end, fastening ribbon to needle.

Beginning and Ending with Ribbon: To begin, fold ribbon end back about 1/4" and pierce both layers with needle; pull ribbon through to form a knot. To end, knot ribbon on wrong side of fabric.

Using a Laying Tool: Using a laying tool gives you a "small hand" to manipulate the ribbon with while stitching. You can use it to hold the ribbon in place, or to help keep the ribbon smooth. You can use a large tapestry needle or a specially designed "trolley" needle as a laying tool.

Silk Ribbon Specialty Stitches

Couched Ribbon Bow – Stitch center of ribbon to fabric. Tie ribbon into a bow. Arrange ribbon loops and streamers as desired and anchor with French Knots.

Gathered Rose – Thread one needle with ribbon and a second needle with matching thread. Bring both needles up at 1 (rose center). Using the "thread" needle, stitch a running stitch for about 1" along one long edge of ribbon. Gently gather ribbon; tack in place. Repeat running stitch and gathering ribbon, tacking ribbon in place around rose center.

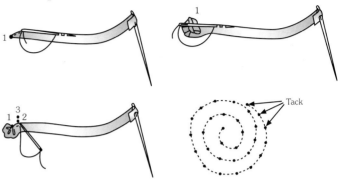

Japanese Ribbon Stitch – Come up at 1. Lay ribbon flat on fabric and go down at 2, piercing ribbon. Gently pull needle through to back. Do not pull ribbon too tightly.

Loop Stitch – Come up at 1. Use laying tool to hold ribbon flat on fabric. Go down at 2, using tool to hold the ribbon flat while pulling ribbon through to back of fabric. Leave tool in loop until needle is brought up at 3 for next loop. Continue in this manner forming desired number of loops.

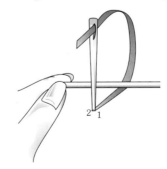 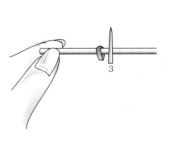

Substitutions

Almost any embroidery stitch can be worked using silk ribbon. However, the specialty stitches can be substituted in many instances to give your work variety and depth. The following list gives you suggestions for some places where you may wish to change the stitches on the original Blocks to specific silk ribbon stitches. This list is by no means complete and is only limited by your imagination!

Lazy daisy petals – Possible substitutions:
- straight stitch
- loop stitch
- Japanese ribbon stitch

Satin stitch flower petals – Possible substitutions:
- loop stitch

Straight stitch flower petals – Possible substitutions:
- straight stitch – use fewer straight stitches than shown on pattern
- Japanese ribbon stitch

Lazy daisy leaves – Possible substitution:
- Japanese ribbon stitch

Small buttonhole wheels – Possible substitution:
- gathered rose

French knots – Work same as with floss, using wider ribbon or more wraps for larger knots.

Large buttonhole wheel - Possible substitution:
- Outline stitch rose – Use ribbon and begin at center; work outline stitch in a dense spiral, making stitches longer as you work to the outside.

Woven rose – Work same as with floss, except use matching floss for spokes and ribbon for weaving.

Silk Garden Wall Hanging
(Photo, pg. 11)

Pat's Pointer: As a general guide, I used floss when working all stems and seam-covering stitches in this wall hanging. Beyond that, I worked out the blocks by eye, substituting silk ribbon and specialty stitches as I felt were good for the overall balance.

Supplies
Fabrics
    6 beige and cream cottons (1/2 yd each)
    1 yd for border and binding
    1 1/2 yds for backing
Silk ribbon
    4mm – purple, coral, rose, 2 pinks, cream, blue, green
    7mm – pink, cream, variegated pink, variegated blue, variegated coral
Floss
    3 greens, cream, beige, 3 pinks, 2 blues, purple
Embellishments
    Multicolor pearl beads
    Multicolor seed beads
Other supplies
    48" square of low-loft batting

Description
Twenty-five paper-pieced blocks (pg. 2) were embroidered using Blocks 1-5 (pg. 4-8). The blocks were sewn together in five rows of five blocks. A feather stitch was worked along seamlines between blocks. It was made into a wall hanging.

Technique – Wall Hanging Finishing

Use a 1/4" seam allowance for all stitching.

1. Cut four 5¹/₂" x 43" border strips. Center and pin one border strip to top edge of quilt top. Beginning and ending ¹/₄" from edges of quilt top, stitch border strip in place. Repeat for each strip.

2. Fold one corner of quilt top diagonally, matching edges. Use a ruler to mark diagonal seamline. Pin, then stitch borders together along drawn line. Trim seam allowance to ¹/₄" and press. Repeat for each corner.

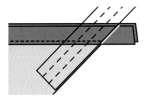 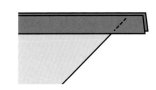

3. Work feather stitch along inner edge of border.

4. Layer and baste backing, batting, and quilt top together (pg. 19).

5. Hand quilt (pg. 19) ¹/₄" inside edges of Section B on each block, ¹/₄" from inner edge of border, and in diagonal lines spaced 1" apart on border.

6. Bind quilt (pg. 19) using a 2¹/₂"w bias strip.

7. Sew seed beads, evenly spaced, along quilting lines on border.

8. Cut a 3" x 40" piece of backing fabric for hanging sleeve. Press edges ¹/₂" to wrong side. Slipstitch long edges to top center back of wall hanging.

Finishing Techniques

QUILTING

Layering and Basting

1. Place batting on wrong side of backing; smooth out batting. Place quilt top right side up on batting.

2. To baste layers together, hand-baste if project will be hand quilted, or pin-baste if project will be machine quilted. Beginning at the center and working toward the edges, use very long stitches (or large safety pins) to baste all layers together horizontally and vertically.

3. Regardless of which quilting method you use, hand baste along outer edges of quilt top through all layers.

Hand Quilting

1. Place center of quilt in a quilting hoop. Check to make sure all layers are smooth.

2. To quilt, thread a quilting needle with an 18-20" length of quilting thread; knot end. Work from center to outer edges. To begin stitching, insert needle on right side of project top approximately ¹/₂" from where you wish to begin quilting. Bring needle up at point you wish to begin; when knot catches on project top, give thread a quick, short pull to pop knot through fabric into batting. Stitch using a small running stitch, making sure stitches secure all layers. To end stitching, tie a small knot close to fabric and pop knot into batting; clip thread close to fabric.

3. When you have finished quilting, remove all basting except outer basting lines. Trim batting and backing even with project top.

Machine Quilting

1. Wind your sewing machine bobbin with general-purpose thread that matches the quilt backing. Do not use quilting thread. Thread the needle of your machine with thread to match quilt top. Set the stitch length for 6-10 stitches per inch and attach the walking foot to sewing machine.

2. Leaving the area exposed where you will place your first line of quilting, roll up each edge of the quilt to help reduce the bulk, keeping fabrics smooth.

3. Use very short stitches for the first ¹/₄" to "lock" beginning of quilting line. Stitch across project, using one hand on each side of the walking foot to slightly spread the fabric and to guide the fabric through the machine. Remove pins as needed. Lock stitches at end of quilting line.

4. When finished quilting, remove remaining pins.

Binding

1. Using width measurement given in project instructions, cut a bias strip of fabric to fit around project, piecing as necessary.

2. Press one end of strip 1/2" to wrong side. Press strip in half lengthwise, wrong sides together.

3. Beginning with pressed end, pin raw edge of binding to quilt front. Stitch in place, using seam allowance given in instructions. Fold pressed edge of binding over to back of quilt and slipstitch in place.

MAKING A KNIFE-EDGE PILLOW

1. Sew pillow front and back together, leaving an opening for turning.

2. Turn pillow right side out; press.

3. Stuff pillow with fiberfill and sew opening closed.

MAKING A WELTED AND RUFFLED PILLOW

1. Follow Steps 1-3 of Making a Welted Pillow (this page) to cut pillow back and add welting.

2. To determine length of ruffle fabric, measure outer dimensions of pillow top and multiply by 2. To determine width of ruffle fabric, multiply the finished width measurement given in project instructions by 2 and add 1" if using 1/2" seam allowance (add 1/2" if using 1/4" seam allowance). Cut a strip of fabric the determined measurements, piecing if necessary.

3. Sew short edges of ruffle together to form a large circle. Fold ruffle in half, matching wrong sides and raw edges. Baste 1/2" and 1/4" from raw edge of ruffle. Pin ruffle to pillow top, pulling threads to draw up gathers to fit pillow top. Baste in place.

4. Stitching as close as possible to welting, sew pillow top and back together, leaving an opening for turning. Turn pillow right side out; press. Stuff with fiberfill and sew final closure by hand.

MAKING A WELTED PILLOW

1. Cut pillow back same size as pillow top.

2. To make welting, measure outer dimensions of pillow top and add 2". Cut a 2 1/2"w bias strip of fabric the determined measurement, piecing if necessary. Lay cord along center of bias strip on wrong side of fabric; fold strip over cord. Using a zipper foot, machine baste along length of strip close to cord. Trim seam allowance to 1/2".

3. Beginning and ending 2" from ends of cording, baste welting to right side of pillow top, clipping seam allowances at corners to allow welting to lie flat. Leaving needle in fabric, cut off one end of welting so it overlaps the other end by 1". Remove 1" of stitching from loose end of welting. Holding fabric away from cord, cut cord so ends butt together. Fold loose end of fabric under 1/2", lap it around other end, and continue stitching welting to pillow top.

4. Stitching as close as possible to welting, sew pillow top and back together, leaving an opening for turning. Turn pillow right side out; press. Stuff with fiberfill and sew final closure by hand.

Production team: Technical writer - Sherry O'Connor. Art - Dana Vaughn. Editorial - Hope Turner. Designer - Linda Tiano.

Pattern testers: Glenda Taylor, Pat Johnson, Sherry O'Connor, and Karen Tyler.